HELLO MY NAME IS OVERCOMER

ANDREKA WALKER

MY SCRIBE PUBLISHING

Copyright © 2023 by Andreka Walker All rights reserved.

No part of this book may be reproduced in any form or by any electronic or mechanical means, including information storage and retrieval systems, without written permission from the author, except for the use of brief quotations in a book review.

ISBN: 978-1-7379354-4-5

Printed in United States

CONTENTS

Acknowledgments — vii
Preface — xi

1. Coming From Where I'm From — 1
2. Beware Of The Dog — 8
3. Valley Days And Better Nights — 21
4. New Life In The A — 26
5. I Do, But I Wish I Didn't — 33
6. My Mr. Right — 45
7. Brayden's NICU Journey — 51
8. Graced In Grief — 86
9. The Promise After The Storm — 91
10. It's A Matter Of The Heart — 97

Overcomer — 113

To my beautiful, strong, God-fearing mother, Idella Lofton…

Thank you for being you & always pushing me to my greatest potential. Since day one you've been there for me. You've always been my inspiration & motivation for what a hard-working, God-fearing woman looks like. You have always been a woman of great integrity & I'm grateful to follow your lead. You raised 5 children & you did it gracefully. You're an example of how to train up a child in the way they should go & when they're old they won't depart. You were not perfect as none of us are but you raised us while being a single parent, doing the best you could & giving it all you could. I'd say you did a fantastic job by God's grace. When things got rough, you never

gave up. I admire your strong indescribable faith in God even in the hard times. You raised us in the ways of the Lord & that means so much. You stressed the importance of us having a relationship with God. Know that your best days are ahead of you. You haven't seen nothing yet! Eyes have not seen nor ears heard nor has it entered into the heart of man the things God has for you. I honor the God in you.
Love you, mom.

ACKNOWLEDGMENTS

I would like to acknowledge my loving mother, Idella Lofton for her prayers & support throughout the years. She would ask me every time we spoke, "Are you done with the book?"

She was that driving force & motivation from start to finish. I've watched you sacrifice a lot for all of your children. You are the most genuine person I know. Thank you for not only talking about Jesus but living Him. I'm beyond blessed to be your daughter.

My loving husband, Brandon Pettis, thank you for being there to support my dreams. You never let up on staying on me to finish the book to its completion. I appreciate you being in my corner when I needed to vent about everything. You never talked over me. You listened and supported me throughout this entire process. I love you so much. In spite of everything we've been through we are still standing by the grace of God. I love you, babe.

My Bishop Roderick Mitchell for the inspiration, word, and wisdom he has poured into my life for over 30 years. Thank you for being a man of integrity and after God's own heart. You're a rare jewel to the world and I'm honored to know you! You live Jesus & not just preach him. I praise God for you and the anointing you carry. Every time I've needed you… you have been there. Not only have you given good words of encouragement, but you've given God's word of encouragement. Continue to preach and teach God's word. The world needs the God in you. I appreciate you!

My eldest sister, Yulonda Edwards for your input, fresh ideas, and always being there when I had questions and needed advice. You're one of the most creative people I know. You have always been an inspiration to me. I appreciate years and years of support. I'm glad to call you sister.

My soul sistas & friends: Trishaun Goodman, Kimberly Johnson, Gingee Honore, and Sharlyne Sobers for continuously pushing me & pouring into my life. I've watched you pray & speak life into this book. I value your friendship and sisterhood.

To my publisher, Shemika Washington of My Scribe Publishing, thank you for all of your support & patience to get the book completed. You poured into my spirit words of encouragement. This wasn't just a project but ministry. I am truly grateful. Thank you for valuing the gift.

To all of my family & loved ones who have been there for me over the years…

I love you all & I appreciate you.

PREFACE

For years I've wanted to write this book. It seemed as if every time I tried to finish, something would prevent completion. The first time I'd written about my life on paper as a teen, I couldn't tell you what happened to it. The most recent time I'd finished the book and sent it as a confidential email, but could no longer find it. I'll never forget the last time writing was on 4/27/2019. I had to start all over but there was so much to be added. The best thing about writing about your life is — it's your life and no one can tell your story like you can. As the word of God says, all things are made beautiful in HIS timing (Ecc. 3:11). So, here we go...

CHAPTER 1
COMING FROM WHERE I'M FROM

I DIDN'T HAVE it easy growing up in the small town of Mound Bayou, MS. I was raised by a single mother of five because my father chose to walk out on my mom when I was two. One day he decided that he couldn't handle the responsibility of a wife, children, and the pressures of life, so he just left. When this happened, my mom had to rebuild her life with the help of our family, church, and loved ones. Although she had support, she lost the home she'd worked very hard to get. I remember us having to live with my aunt until mom could get back on her feet.

We eventually moved into a three-bedroom apartment in The Banks Edition. Yep! My mom, along with her four girls and only son were forced to fit into three bedrooms. My brother had his own room, and we girls slept in the other. We all shared one bathroom. Although we didn't have a lot, we had each other.

I have so many memories growing up in Mound Bayou, some good, and some bad. I remember mom working extremely hard to do everything she could for us. Once my two oldest siblings graduated and moved away, we began to stay home with my second oldest sister. My older siblings were like a second set of parents, but this sister was something else back then. When my mom went to work, sis would have boys in and out of the apartment. I recall a time when the guys made my little sister and I feel super uncomfortable and would say really sexually inappropriate things to us. I was young, but I wasn't naive.

My friends and I would often play "Hide & Go Get It" just for fun. However, something felt very uncomfortable about those older guys saying the things they would say to us. For years, we never told anyone about it. I had no idea that this mindset of keeping secrets about inappropriate older men was a dangerous seed that would grow.

What I knew at the time was that my mom already had enough on her plate. She worked at a plant for years to make ends meet for us. Outside of work, my mom's life revolved around ministry and church. I remember she would host Bible studies in our neighborhood for the children. She was a light to the community and is well respected to this day.

We were always in church, so I'm being literal when I say I grew up in church. We were under the leadership of Bishop Roderick Mitchell and transitioned from Mount Pilgrim Missionary Baptist Church to The New Life Church. I eventually joined the choir at church and recognized that I was gifted in music. I would stand in front of the mirror saying to myself, " I'm going to sing like Shirley Caesar one day." I loved music. It was my go-to even though my mom would only let us listen to Gospel. My first time singing publicly was at the groundbreaking of my childhood church. I wasn't the most well-behaved child, but I wasn't too terrible either. I remember my mom caught me sticking up my middle finger and I thought she'd forgotten by the time we got home. Let's just say, I'll never forget that day or the whooping I got.

During the time mom worked at a factory, she got into a new relationship and we eventually moved from Mound Bayou to Cleveland, MS. I was heading to the 7th grade. I was really excited about the move. I began school at Eastwood Junior High School. It felt good to be in a house for a change too. My stepdad was actually pretty cool, but I still gave him hell at times. My first year in Cleveland was a smooth transition, but things took a turn after I was promoted to 8th grade.

I was introduced to all kinds of stuff from that point on. One day my sister and I went to visit my older cousin at her house. When we were in her room, she showed us a bag of all sorts of condoms. I'd never seen anything like it. That one visit was when it all started. She told us about a lot of sexual experiences she had been involved in and at that time she was "out there!" Unfortunately, I was intrigued by it.

Soon after introducing me to her world, she linked me with this guy she knew. I was thirteen and he was in high school. I started talking to him over the phone and eventually, I snuck him into our house. I was so curious about this life that my cousin made seem so cool. So yeah... he snuck in for one reason and we had sex. It was my first time and I felt that it wasn't all that it was hyped up to be. We just had sex and he left. I was so naive at the time. I really thought it was supposed to be special, but nope it wasn't at all. What it did do was open some new doors in my life.

I felt terrible because my late grandmother had warned me about having sex the previous year. They say warning comes before destruction, but I didn't take heed. Having sex that one time turned me into a sex addict. I kept having sex with him, then I eventually met someone else. I actually formed a "relationship" with the next guy. I thought I was special to him. Yet in the end, it was really all about sex for him.

Many people thought I was this smart and quiet girl but I was fighting so many internal battles. I was walking down the hall one day at school and a condom fell out of my pocket while the principal walked by. I just knew I was in trouble. My mom never found out about it, and he just gave me a warning.

Although I was going down this new road of sexual misconduct, I was killing it academically. I successfully completed junior high school as the salutatorian of my class. Coming from where I'm from, all I had to do was make good grades and not get caught. I did a good job with that until one day my actions caught up with me. What I had been doing in the dark was brought to light.

CHAPTER 2
BEWARE OF THE DOG

BY THE TIME I got to high school, I was more than sexually active. I was out there! Just like my cousin, if not worse! My behavior just kept getting worse. My mom had us in church almost every single day. I lived the life of a preacher's kid. We were in the church at least 3 days out of the week, every single week. The foundation of God's Word was and has always been inside me, but I had completely lost my way at this point.

One day I was walking to the store and this older guy saw me and told me he loved my jacket. He asked me if he could buy it. If you know me, you know I've always been a hustler, so I sold it to him. He gave me his number and told me to call him sometime. I was impressed by the wad of money he flashed in front of me and how cool he was, so I did. He and I hung out a few times, and I ended up skipping school to be with him. Instantly, it was like he had a hold on me. It made me feel good to be "taken care of." It was like he was filling a void that I didn't know was there. We had sex once and it was one of the biggest mistakes of my life.

Days later, I began to feel sick. I went to the doctor and found out he'd given me trichomoniasis and chlamydia. I felt disgusted with myself that I allowed myself to get entangled with this grown man who gave me an STD. It only took one time! I asked him about it and of course, he denied it, but he was the only one I was with at that time. I went back for a follow-up about a week later, and after taking the meds, both diseases were cleared up. I tried so hard to cut this guy off, but he was a jerk. He stalked me for a while until he realized I was seriously done. That was my first and last time sleeping with him.

I slowed down after the situation blew over. A couple of months after that, I was laying in the tub and while sitting there I began to bleed heavily. The tub was full of blood. My mom was working, so I had my stepdad take me to the emergency room. I found out I was having a miscarriage— I was about four months pregnant with a girl. I had no idea that I was pregnant! It didn't show when I'd gone to the doctor previously because it was too early to detect. I sat in the hospital that night feeling like crap! I was only fourteen and had lost a child. I lived with that guilt for years. While writing this, I think of how I would've had an eighteen-year-old if she'd lived. I was too afraid to communicate with the child's father because I was honestly afraid of him and didn't want to have anything to do with him after I found out about him giving me the STD. The situation was already messy. Although I was wrong for allowing myself to get entangled with him, he had committed many wrongs too. He was eight years older than me.

I remained focused for a while, but I eventually got distracted again. I dated and became sexually involved here and there. I really wish I had gone to counseling at the time. I still attended church regularly…I was there but wasn't there. I had low self-esteem that started when I was very young, wishing my father was there to protect me. I was truly broken, lost, and confused. I felt like an embarrassment, although hardly anyone knew what I had gone through. Instead of getting help and dealing with the issues, I got introduced to smoking, drinking, partying, and hustling.

I spent every summer in Georgia with my oldest sister, and I was no better there. I really showed out almost every year. I even ran away a few times. I started to engage in online dating. Although I was never sexually active with anyone I met online, I put my family at risk by trying to meet up with one of the guys. Thankfully, he wasn't a psychopath and my sister found out what I'd been doing. She called the guy and told him my real age. It totally freaked him out. My sister was adamant about sending me to boot camp, but I just wanted to go home. I gave her such a hard time. She literally gave us anything we wanted.

My sister created opportunities for us to be able to experience and be exposed to so many things that we didn't have access to living in a small town. Anything I ever wanted, she came through for me, but it wasn't enough. Even when I returned home, I ran away for a couple of days at a time. I don't know what I was thinking. I came from a loving family with a nice room of my own but chose to be in the streets sleeping on floors with roaches and getting high.

My sister wasn't the only person who went out of their way to be there for me and try to steer me in the right direction. I remember Ms. Fountaine, one of my childhood mentors, would help my mom look for me when I ran away. I will always remember this instance when she drove behind me trying to encourage me to get in the car with her and go home. She literally took me under her wing and tried to help me.

I got in trouble for many things, but I didn't bother anybody. I had church friends that I called my church crew–my little sister, Zakiya, and Kamara. We had so much fun in church and outside of church. Those were my riders! I went to this step show with them one night. This one girl kept picking on me. She disliked me because of a boy we both dealt with. The DJ messed around and played, "Lean With it, Rock With It" and it was over with. I beat her out of her shirt and bra.

She brought the drama to the school bus, and this time my sister jumped in and fought her too. Then, she caught my sister off guard and fought her in the cafeteria. When I found out, I was getting off the VoTech school bus. I ran off the bus like I was Madea. (I had really big boobs — they called me titty city). I found the girl and beat her down again. She tried to stab me but that didn't stop me from whooping her. Unfortunately, our principal called the police and we were arrested. I remember them trying to take my picture for a mugshot. I told them to hold on and let me get my lip gloss—smh. Thankfully, the charges were dropped after a few phone calls. The first person we called was one of our family and church members – Ms.

Jori Weeks. I'll never forget her because she had our back. We didn't get a legal record, but we did get suspended from school for two weeks. I just knew my mom was gonna be upset. But mama knew we didn't bother anyone and we'd just gotten tired of constantly being picked on. Years went on and I kept doing the same old crazy things and at this point, I was only doing just enough to get by in my classes. I was no longer anything like the focused salutatorian from junior high school because I simply didn't care anymore.

In my senior year of high school, I met an older guy who lived thirty minutes away from me. We weren't sexually active or romantically involved. Our relationship was strictly business. I looked up to him because he was making money. I learned so much about street life from being around him. He came off as if he wanted to be my mentor, but it was too late once I realized he had other motives. One day we were at the trap hotel and that's when our so-called friendship took a turn for the worse.

We'd gotten really high and drunk that night. I remember laying down because I didn't have the strength to move. I was basically out of it. He came and stood over me, then started touching me aggressively. When he came at me like that, it completely shocked me because I'd never been attracted to him sexually nor had he ever given me the slightest hint that he wanted to be sexual with me. I remember begging and pleading with him to please leave me alone. He wouldn't take no for an answer. I trembled in fear as he gripped me and pinned me down on the bed and pulled out his penis and began raping me. I felt so helpless. I was so intoxicated and high that I didn't have the strength mentally or physically to get this grown man who was 6'7 with a stocky build off of me.

I begged and pleaded for him to stop as tears fell from my face. I fought so hard to get him off of me, but I couldn't overpower him. I screamed as loud as I could, but no one heard me. I thought I could trust this man. He was on so many drugs that I should've known his intent with me was no good. He became angrier with me for trying to escape his grip. I'd never been so afraid in my life. I really thought he was going to kill me. All I saw was rage on his face. I kept begging him to please let me go, but he didn't until he was finished.

His phone rang, and that's what saved me. He made me get up and threw me out of the room to the ground and left me there stranded. He got in his car and sped off. I was so embarrassed. I called so many people that night until I had no other choice but to call my mother. I was so afraid of what she might do to me because it was so late and I'd snuck out of the house. She came and got me from where I was. It was an awkward ride home. I felt so betrayed and disgusted with myself. I told her what had happened and apologized over and over. She didn't fuss. She didn't judge me, but she prayed for me.

That was the absolute scariest night of my life. I was too afraid of this man because of his strong reputation in the streets. I wanted to give his name and report it to the police for years but was afraid to. He would drive by my job and threaten to hurt my family if I ever told anyone. I felt that if I brought attention to it, no one would believe me and would wonder why I was there in the first place. To this day, I wish I'd spoken up because I'm sure he's raped other young girls.

I went through counseling to help me with my sanity after that happened. I'd never experienced anything like that before. No, I wasn't a virgin, and yes I'd dealt with promiscuity, but never had I ever been forced to have sex with someone. I beat myself up for a while. I felt like maybe I deserved it. It was my fault because I shouldn't have snuck out of the house that night. The drugs and money weren't worth the trauma that I experienced. I started to really see the reality that the streets didn't love me.

My mom knew I needed help and set me up to start counseling with my pastor. I will never forget his words. He gave the example of a "beware of the dog" sign. He said that once you crossed the lines of where you're not welcome and ignored that warning sign, then at that point the "dogs" would do as they pleased with you. He gave me another example of what it would be like to go back to those old ways. He said that going back to the lifestyle would be like vomiting and picking it back up and putting it in my mouth. Although it was very detailed and disgusting, I think about that example every time I want to go back to what God delivered me from. I continued counseling and it made a huge difference. I was afraid to have sex with anyone after that horrific night. I hate it took that night to slow me down, but I'm grateful that I became better. I re-dedicated my life to Christ and was ready for a fresh start.

Trying to live the street life, running away, and being rebellious caused me to fall out of love with my passion. I decided to reconnect with what I loved—music. I joined the high school choir and became a lead vocalist. My favorite song to lead was *"Create In Me A Clean Heart"* and it is still my favorite song today. Lord knows I needed Him to restore my joy. My love for music and joining the choir led me to a full scholarship at Mississippi Valley State University. I went through a lot in my high school days, but God had already prepared and paid for the start of a new me.

CHAPTER 3
VALLEY DAYS AND BETTER NIGHTS

COLLEGE YEARS WERE the first time in years I'd ever been so focused on academics, becoming a better me, and pleasing God. Those years of going to church every week, and sitting under the word weren't in vain. In the words of Bishop Mitchell, "I am going with God. It doesn't matter who it separates me from or identifies me with, I'm going with God." I'd been through so much growing up, I felt that it was time to be sold out for Christ. I also made the conscious decision to forgive my father. God rekindled our relationship and my father even told me he loved me for the first time in my life.

God used me to share my story with a lot of young people on campus. I worked as a resident assistant throughout my years at MVSU. I partnered with the youth pastor at my home church to do motivational seminars called, "Too Young To Die For Love." The seminars brought awareness to intimate partner violence, promoted abstinence, and motivated young people to avoid destructive choices and habits. I met so many young women who shared deep levels of trauma that happened to them growing up and on campus. In those moments, I realized that college wasn't about just an education but it was an assignment. God used my mess to be a message to those young women. They felt comfortable speaking to me because I'd already experienced what they were going through. God opened many doors of opportunities for me. I traveled to many places with the university choir and met some of the most amazing people! I had the opportunity to travel to Nassau, Bahamas to sing. I can honestly say college was a new start for me.

My mission was ministry. Although I did enjoy myself and go to a party every now and then, I can say that I touched so many lives on that campus and brought so many to know Jesus. It felt good to finally grow and be a better person. I'll be honest, I had a couple of drawbacks here and there.

A major challenge for me was when I found out my niece passed away. This unexpected and devastating news turned my world upside down. I remember traveling to West Virginia with my family. I went out one night with them and got sloppy drunk. It was so bad that I missed my flight the following day and had to ride back with my aunt. I was truly hurt about my niece's death, but I also felt guilty and beat myself up for a while because I'd temporarily lost focus. I asked God to please forgive me for my downfall. I was so focused on what I was not doing right when I should've just focused on things God had already made right within me and continually grow from there. We can beat ourselves up sometimes about our shortcomings and forget how far God has brought us. Though we fall, we are not utterly cast down. I had to move forward from that. God is so gracious that he allowed me to move past it and continue to do his work.

I met this guy in the military during my college days, and he was such a great guy. Our friendship meant the world to me. Whenever I needed anything, he came through. It was such a healthy relationship, but it was temporary. I was grateful to have known him. I'd never been treated that well by any man I'd dated previously. Even with that relationship, I was able to stay focused and was blessed to graduate with honors and went on to get my master's degree at Delta State University.

God blessed me with a great-paying job in the finance industry, and I leased my first apartment. I felt like I truly made the people I'd hurt the most (especially my mother and sister) so proud of me. God was literally pouring blessings on me in spite of my past. I had to come to the realization that I was not my past. God still loves me and his ways and plans are higher than mine. After I received my master's degree, I moved to Atlanta.

CHAPTER 4
NEW LIFE IN THE A

ATLANTA WAS TRULY A FAITH WALK! I moved there focused and ready to work. It was hard for me to find employment in the beginning. I was constantly told that I was overqualified or I didn't have enough work experience. I became very discouraged during that time, but I joined my sister's church and immediately became a member of the choir, and eventually started ministering with the praise team. God truly moved and took my gift of music and ministry higher. I was afforded the opportunity to audition for BET's Sunday Best. Although I didn't make it to the show, I met different people there who were blessed by my gift. I sang at weddings and also ministered at several different ministries throughout Metro Atlanta.

I prayed daily but got impatient at times while waiting. I tried to remain focused and stay in the Word. Eight months later, my best friend called and said he had been offered two job positions at different companies and asked me if I wanted one. I thought he was joking, but he was so serious. I got hired through a temp agency and quickly got promoted in months because of my job performance. I was able to move into a nice luxury apartment near one of my favorite malls. I was truly grateful to God, my sister, and my family who took care of me for months until I started working.

One day I saw a Facebook post of an Atlanta pastor preaching and the message truly touched my heart. A couple of people had already told me about this ministry, so I googled it and decided to go visit the church. Service was like a breath of fresh air. My spirit felt as if there was something tugging on me to join, but I was hesitant. I decided to go back a couple more times and each time I felt as though I was in the right place. One Sunday on my way inside the church, I decided to make an encouraging post on Facebook. To my surprise, the pastor started teaching on exactly what I posted. At that point, I knew this would be the Sunday I joined. I sent an email to the church I was attending and let them know I'd be joining another ministry. It was honestly one of the best decisions I made.

After joining the church I began to grow spiritually and became active in ministry. I became a member of the choir and praise team as soon as I got on board. I've always been a faithful tither and as I began to sow seeds into this ministry, I saw more fruit coming forth. One Sunday, my cousin came into town to visit and after church, he introduced me to one of his friends from the military. Small word—the lady he introduced me to was a member of my church and we were both in the choir.

We became friends on Facebook and she invited me to her housewarming party. When I got there, I was so excited to celebrate with her in her new home. I told her I'd thought about buying a home one day. She encouraged me to do so and told me to go talk to her boyfriend who was a realtor. I talked with him about my desire to purchase a home. He gave me his card and told me when I was ready to let him know. Months later, I reached out to him. I didn't move on things immediately because it was such a major decision and I wasn't sure I was one hundred percent ready. I eventually got past all of the uncertainty and started the home-buying process. Right in the middle of everything, the unexpected happened. My mom was diagnosed with cancer. I will never forget the day she called my phone. I was sitting in my car when she told me she'd been diagnosed.

I've gotten some bad news in my lifetime, but that was one of the hardest phone calls I've ever received. I encouraged her that everything would be fine and to keep her head up. When I got off the phone, I sat in my car and cried for a whole hour. I felt numb and knew that I would have to find the strength to get home. I wrestled with sleeping the whole night. My thoughts were running rampant and I knew I'd have to get myself together. I began to pray and ask God to help me be strong for her. My mom moved to Atlanta during that time for treatment at Emory. She had several appointments and I was able to go to a few with her. While this was going on, I was trying to finalize the home-buying process. Sometimes you have to walk the journey alone and trust God and know that timing is everything.

I finally decided to tell my family about the great news in hopes of bringing some joy into our lives in the midst of the difficult situation we were in as a family. I will never forget my mom's reaction. She was so excited for me. At that moment, I knew that it was God's plan. I remember the day my family came over and did a walk-through with me. It was such an emotional time. When my mom saw the house, she said she instantly knew in her spirit that it was in God's will. She felt the presence of God. She prayed and blessed my home in the midst of her health condition. That day was truly amazing. I always prayed to buy a new home by the age of thirty. God did it for me sooner and I am forever grateful!

The following month, my mom had to have a mastectomy. I remember the day she came out of her surgery and we all shed a few tears of gratitude. We have all heard the saying, "You look like nothing you've gone through." Well, that was my mom as she began recovery. She looked NOTHING like what she'd just experienced. She was walking the halls of the hospital singing, "Look what the Lord has done. He healed my body, he touched my mind. He saved me just in time. I'm going to praise him. Look what the Lord has done." Her faith in God did not waiver throughout her entire journey.

CHAPTER 5
I DO, BUT I WISH I DIDN'T

DURING THE TIME that my mother was battling breast cancer, I started talking to this guy who had just finished school and was in Atlanta visiting his cousin. We talked for hours and hours non-stop for a couple of weeks so I felt very comfortable with him by the time we went on our first date. We dined at my favorite restaurant, Joe's Crab Shack. After our date, he came over to the house and I went upstairs and got comfy. I came back downstairs in a onesie. It was pretty cold outside that day, but we went outside to the backyard. We sat down and I lay there in his arms as he held me. We sat there and talked for over an hour before we went inside. When we got back inside, he wanted to take it there. He shared how he was feeling toward me. The vibe was definitely right but I explained to him that I was celibate and I only wanted to be with someone who had my best interest at heart.

We continued to date and eventually, he won me over completely. I literally felt like I'd met my superman. It was as if he came into my life at the perfect time. He was there for me while I watched my mom battle cancer. I wasn't in a good place mentally or spiritually at that time. My mom and I are very close and she means so much to me. In all honesty, I battled depression heavily. We eventually got married, but it was way too soon. The marriage didn't last long at all. We went through counseling and he continued to lie to me about any and everything. I checked his phone records and kept seeing the same New York number. Back then you could put the number in Facebook and see if it was attached to your account, so I did a little investigating. Of course, the number belonged to some random female. I asked him about her, but he denied knowing her.

One day, I called the New York number and it was definitely the chick from Facebook. She didn't hold anything back. She said she had no idea that he was married. She informed me that they'd been dating and having unprotected sex. He'd even taken her to a few of his family events. This man was out of control on so many levels. She said they met online. I literally took notes during our conversation because, at that moment, I knew I was done with him and would subpoena her if I needed to for court. I was mad hot, but he didn't even come home that night. I got in my car with intense rage in my heart and went to his friend's place. I got out of the car and started banging on the door. I was screaming, acting a fool, and completely out of character. His friend told me he wasn't there and that I needed to leave, but I was so angry that I just sat in the car and waited for him to show up. I sat outside of the apartment complex hurt, angry, and looking like a fool late into the wee hours of the next morning. He never showed up.

I had to go to work a few hours after I left his friend's place. I drove to the Walmart nearby, got some underwear, clothes, and personal items, and joined L. A. Fitness to shower. I sat in the sauna for about an hour first and cried my eyes out. I went to work looking like a zombie because I hadn't slept.

Days passed, and this man had basically disappeared on me. He apologized to me through text. I decided within my heart that I was over it. During that time, my cousin had asked me to sing at her wedding. Even though I was in so much emotional pain, I sacrificed and drove to Memphis to sing. After I finished, I went back to my hotel room and balled, crying because I had to go back home and deal with my own mess of a marriage. I decided to get a divorce.

I discussed it with him and he refused to go along with it. I went over to give him the papers to look over and his friend answered the door and said, "Get over it, all men cheat. You know he loves you." I responded with a few choice words and left. The next day I found one of the most successful attorneys in Georgia, paid cash money, and requested he be served. Yep! I had him served at his job.

The ghost man (my ex-husband) resurfaced and he was pissed! I asked him for weeks to sign the divorce papers which would have saved him money, but he refused. At that point, he called daily begging me not to leave him. He even showed up at my job crying in the parking lot. I told him if he wanted to speak to me, he needed to contact my attorney. He was always in between jobs, so I knew he couldn't afford an attorney. The grounds for divorce was adultery and I was prepared to prove it. I'd found out about several more women during the whole process. He knew he couldn't deny it. He agreed to sign the documents and I was granted EVERYTHING I asked for. I received the final divorce decree and it was a breath of fresh air. I decided to focus on my healing.

I was able to put on a strong front in order to protect myself, but deep down, I was struggling with the hurt from everything that happened. Marrying the wrong person and having to go through a divorce had always been a fear of mine. My father married and divorced four times, and there I was in the same predicament. I literally felt like a failure.

I'd practiced years of celibacy only to wait for marriage to finally have sex, but I married the wrong man. I went through a stage of being upset with God that lasted for quite a while. In actuality, it was all my fault. I married a man in haste because of my own vulnerability. The marriage wasn't ordained by God. I was in pain when I met him. My favorite person on the planet, my mom, was battling cancer. I thought he was a blessing during that time, but he was actually a distraction.

Instead of getting counseling, I ran to other things. For months, I was hurt and disappointed. I got on a dating app and would go on several dates to enjoy the meal and company. Dating was no longer a means to meet my future husband, but it became a form of entertainment for me. Then, I developed an addiction to marijuana. I was indulging in it in every form— smoking, eating edibles, and even drinking the liquid form.

Waiting for marriage for sex wasn't even a thought in my mind. I'd done that already but that didn't work out for me.

My thoughts were rooted in rebellion against God. I became sexually involved with this one guy I'd met online. He was literally buying me everything I wanted and paying my bills. The divorce left me in a financial bind, and he was ready and willing to help me in any way I needed him to. I enjoyed the lustful relationship with him, but it wasn't long before I became bored. Eventually, the situation grew toxic and I had to block him. Although he was a huge help financially, we never went on dates or anything. He fulfilled my sexual pleasures as I did his.

I was going through it and I literally felt like I was sinking in my sins. I'd leave the church, go home, and smoke until I passed out. I remember one weekend, I had a girl's night! I invited a few of my friends over and we went out for a night out on the town. I got sloppy drunk, and was beyond wasted! We came back home and my friends were looking for me. I was crying, hysterical, and fell asleep in my closet. I still have the videos from that night, and it's almost unbelievable. I still look at them and say…Wow!

The next morning, we all got up for church. I was so hungover that I couldn't tell you what my pastor preached about. After service, it was raining and one of my friends asked me to grab her umbrella. I told her to give me a second and she snapped! Her words were, "If it was IG, (my ex-husband) you would've done it" and she began to go on this rant and patronize me about my relationship with him. All I could hear was pure jealousy coming out of her mouth but because we were on church grounds, I held my peace. The ride home from church was a wild one though. My other friend was trying to diffuse the situation as best as she could. I was already hurting and this supposed friend tried to tear me down. I told her to get her stuff from my home and to never contact me again.

It shocked me that she tried to kick me while I was already down. She tried contacting me for a while, but I never responded. It goes to show you how at times you have people closest to you who may envy your life. It was hurtful to know that she was jealous of me the entire time I was married. She showed her true colors and I had no room for that in my life. She eventually sent me an email apologizing for her behavior. She said she was in one of the darkest places in her life and felt so alone in what she was going through, but that was no excuse for the way she treated me. She went on to say I was her best friend and she hoped I'd forgive her. I forgave her but kept my distance because I was still knee-deep in my own battles.

One day I remember drinking a full bottle of liquid marijuana. Then, I got in my car and drove to Joe's Crab Shack. By the time I made it to the parking lot, the drink kicked in. I sat in the parking lot and cried so hard. It was at that moment I realized I needed help. I called my best friend and wept, telling her how I'd been struggling with depression and getting high to suppress the hurt.

After that conversation, I started therapy and got the professional help I needed to cope with everything that I had been through. At that time, divorce felt worse than losing someone to death. What made it feel worse was that he made the choice to disrespect me and our marriage. I had to forgive him, move forward, and accept the fact that I made a major move before hearing the voice of God. I was in a state of vulnerability when I met him and missed the warning signs before I married him. I had to forgive myself first, then him.

Months went by and true healing began. I started to really enjoy life again. I was back to doing some of the things I loved… singing, shopping, and traveling. I love the beach so I went there to visit a few times for peace. I lost love, but I was finding myself and my way back to God.

CHAPTER 6
MY MR. RIGHT

ONE DAY my friend from California came to visit and we decided to throw some meat on the grill. He'd brought along his barber friend who asked if he could bring his cousin. I told him I didn't mind. When his cousin got to the house, he introduced us. It was my first time meeting Brandon. He immediately took interest in me. He told me he was a handyman and that if I ever needed anything done to call him. He handed me his business card. I placed it on the couch and honestly had no intention of ever calling. We talked for a few hours at the house and I really enjoyed our conversation. I didn't want to have anything to do with a relationship.

A few days later, I realized one of the guys had left their iPhone at my house. I called my friend and his barber friend on Facebook but didn't get a response. Then I remembered his cousin Brandon that I'd met and called him to see if he lost his iPhone. He said it wasn't his but he'd been waiting for my call. He told me if I hadn't called him in a few days, he was about to start sending me flowers. He was out with his biker friends and quickly asked if he could take me bowling. I told him I wasn't in the mood for it. He then asked if he could take me to the movies. I told him it was cool. He dropped everything he was doing and headed my way. I was thinking this guy isn't playing about taking me on a date. Our first date was really chill and I enjoyed his company. We began to hang out and talk more after that. I was beginning to really dig him.

During that time, I was invited to minister in song at a women's conference. On the day of the event, God truly showed up and showed out. While singing, God had me share my testimony. It literally shifted the atmosphere in the room. Women were crying out before God. The Spirit of God was so strong and God truly moved. When it was time for offering, I heard God say give. It was a sacrificial offering. As I was preparing my seed, the prophetess looked over at me and told me to stand up.

She spoke this word of prophecy over my life:

"Last year couldn't send you to a mental hospital. The enemy has been wanting you to lose your mind for a while now. God says your Boaz is coming. He is going to bless you with a husband and family. God says that he can trust you with money. He sees the seeds that you've sown over the years. You're going to be a multimillionaire. You

will write a best-selling book and you will be the biggest success story in your family. God wants you to tell the raw truth and not hold back."

That was the second time in my life that a prophecy came forward that I'd be a millionaire. I was only a teenager the first time. For years, I stood firm in my belief that one day I'd see it. My voicemail for years has always been, "Hi, you've reached the millionaire. Sorry, I'm unavailable."

God confirmed his word. I'd been feeling the push to write my story since high school but never finished. I would start but never complete it. I took that word and began writing the following week. For months I'd write a little at a time but get distracted and quit. God even gave me the name for my book… *Hello My Name is Overcomer*. I began selling t-shirts to promote the book and everything.

Things were beginning to look up. Although I took occasional pauses from writing, my relationship with Brandon was going well. We took our first trip together to Houston. When I say he spoiled me silly and made sure I didn't have to worry about anything, I mean that. To this day I rarely hear the word, "No." When we came back from Houston. I found out I was pregnant.

I struggled to accept the fact that I was expecting because we hadn't been together that long and we weren't married. I came to terms that children are a gift from God and they are a reward from him. The sin was in the premarital sex, not my baby. I asked God for forgiveness and forgave myself. I began to grow more and more in love with my son and his father.

Brandon didn't miss a beat when it came to providing for us. We made the decision to live together because of fi financial reasons, my high-risk pregnancy, and he wanted to be there to support us. While pregnant, I had to have numerous doctor visits. We found out that we both tested positive for the gene of cystic fibrosis (CF) and there was a twenty-five percent chance our son could have it. I'll be honest it worried me the majority of the pregnancy but I knew God's will would be done. I prayed over my son daily.

We threw this huge baby shower for Brayden. Our family and loved ones came from near and far to support us. My friends and my child's Godmother did a beautiful job with the décor and putting everything together. My son was blessed with so many gifts. We didn't have to buy anything for months. Everything felt perfect…until it didn't.

CHAPTER 7
BRAYDEN'S NICU JOURNEY

A FEW WEEKS later we went to the cabin for Brandon's birthday. It was a very peaceful trip but I hadn't been feeling the best. I kept telling B something felt off. When we got home, I called my OB and told him I wasn't feeling well. I was experiencing discomfort in my stomach. My doctor said I was 32 weeks, so he was confident that it was just constipation. I felt worse as more time passed, so I drove myself to the ER. Shortly after I arrived and checked into the hospital, the nurses informed me that I was dilated, and in what felt like only a few minutes, I was getting prepared to go into labor. I can't explain how nervous I was. I had my husband, mother-in-law, and best friend there for support. Because it was so sudden, they didn't have time to give me an epidural so I felt every ounce of labor pain.

My support system and music were my only sources of comfort throughout my labor and delivery. We were playing worship music — *War* by Charles Jenkins and *Deliver Me* by Donald Lawrence. On December 17, 2019, I gave birth to my firstborn son, Brayden Jahmai Pettis at 10:30 a.m. He weighed four pounds, three ounces, and was seventeen inches long. Baby boy came out screaming at the top of his lungs. I just knew everything would be okay. Because he was premature, we knew he would have to spend some time in NICU. The doctors assured me that because of his weight, he wouldn't have to be there too long. The next day, the doctors were more concerned after evaluating him. Brayden wasn't keeping the food down and was having trouble gaining weight. At that moment I began to document his NICU journey. The first couple of days he was doing fine, but they had to stop feeding him milk and went back to feeding him through an IV because he wasn't digesting the formula as he should. His breathing was fast but still within a normal range.

By the end of the week, they were able to take out his arterial line and resume his milk feedings to evaluate his progress. They stopped the antibiotics because his labs came back fine. His potassium went back to normal. His nurse said that he was very active. As days went by, his breathing got better and his tummy was looking okay but they still watched him closely. As days passed, they took him off the milk again and gave him nutrients through his IVR. They inserted a tube to flush out the air in his belly. On December 23rd, I was informed Brayden had to be transferred to Children's Healthcare of Atlanta for further evaluation. They believed something developed abnormally in his digestive tract. They did additional testing that day to see what was blocking his digestion, but our confession and belief was that all would be well. The new hospital was way better although the drive was long. We did what we had to for our baby boy. We were even able to hold him for the first time! We waited patiently on follow-up X-rays to tell us what the problem was. They planned to do an additional X-ray the next morning while they were waiting for the contrast to move further into his digestive tract so they could visualize it better.

On Christmas Eve, Brayden looked so cute with his Christmas hat. I could tell he was really tired from being up all night. His belly was nice and soft but he wasn't producing stool. Later that day, the doctor informed us that he had some not-so-good news to share. Brayden had been diagnosed with cystic fibrosis with two mutations in his genes. We'd been told while he was in the womb that there was a one in four chance that he could have it. The news didn't shock us but it did disappoint us because by faith we prayed and believed God for a healthy son. Although the news saddened our hearts, we were prepared to take that journey with our son and do whatever was necessary to get him the treatment he needed.

We believed the report of the Lord and knew that by HIS stripes Brayden was healed. We thanked God in advance for his complete healing. We declared that it was not there and God would cancel this out. Although we prayed for healing, we knew that God's will would be done. Our hearts rejoice for what we believed God was going to do. Our confession was that we would see a total victory. Brayden was moved on the fifth day. We knew that five is the number of grace and that God's grace was sufficient for us.

On Christmas Day, we were surrounded by doctors. The Cystic Fibrosis Foundation took us to a room for almost eight hours explaining the condition, the type of CF (Delta F508), and the treatments he would need. There were so many thoughts running through my head as they spoke. My husband and I couldn't believe all the challenges our son would face, but we were going to do whatever. The next day, Brayden finally passed gas for the first time. The doctors wanted to start him on enzymes which are given through eating apple sauce. However, he was not big enough to ingest it. They wanted to be able to establish his feedings and monitor his weight gain. He was finally able to have a bowel movement, which was a major progression for him as it was his first time. They sent his stool in for testing. His weight was up and down for days. On December 30th, Brayden vomited and it caused his heart rate to drop. He began to breathe too fast and they had to give him fluids through his nose again. On New Year's Eve, his condition was about the same. He was breathing really fast but he was able to pass stool. Brayden finally weighed in at five pounds that day.

I left the hospital that night and all I could say was, God you get the glory out of this! I never knew I'd begin the New Year watching my firstborn battling health challenges. He was such a tough little fighter. Every day was literally a faith walk. Some days, we got good news, and some days not so good.

One day, we got a major glimpse of hope. Brayden started to tolerate milk. I remember them letting us feed him with the little bottle for the first time. It was truly a blessing. Later that day, they had to stop the feeding because he spit up. He was breathing so hard that they had to increase his oxygen flow. After days of his bowels not moving, Brayden finally passed gas and stool. He was doing better day by day. He even gained three more ounces. We began to get excited again! His breathing improved, and they increased his feedings again. He was even able to graduate to a big boy crib. I remember singing this song to Brayden, God says.

By HIS stripes — Brayden is healed. By HIS blood — Brayden is healed By HIS word — Brayden is healed.

I continued to declare that he was spiritually, emotionally, and physically healed. Days went by and Brayden was getting better daily. They began to increase his milk volume. My boy was gaining weight and everything. Around mid-January, the doctor told us that Brayden pulled out his own tubes the night before. I believe Brayden saw what was to come. The doctors took out his PICC line and his breathing had gotten tons better. Brayden was beginning to tolerate his feedings more. Days later, doctors were concerned again but this time it was about the color of his stool – it was white. His liver function tests were abnormal.

I began to thank God for his healing power. I declared that every disease had to bow down at the name of Jesus. My husband and I even began fasting and praying for Brayden's complete healing. God spoke to me during the fasting to not be afraid. Psalms 147:3 is the scripture that blessed me: *He heals the brokenhearted and binds up their wounds and that where two or three are gathered- he would be in the midst (Matthew 18:20).*

We had so many prayer warriors on our team. To this day I'm thankful for the support, love, and prayers of so many. I believe that for me, grieving started Brayden's first few days in the NICU. I knew that God was and is a healer as I'd seen him years prior heal my mom from cancer. I stood on his word and that's what gave us strength.

On January 17th, he had more testing. His brain x-ray looked great, and his ultrasound looked fine, as well as his tummy. However, he was diagnosed with cholestasis and had to be started on a new medication. He did well with the medicine and they increased his feedings, but he wasn't gaining or losing weight. They tried feeding him later that day but he threw up. The NICU journey was like a rollercoaster experience. Days later his weight went down.

Then, for days Brayden was doing better and the doctors decided to start him on enzymes toward the end of that month. One day he did well with feedings, but the next day he didn't do as well. By noon, his belly was big and there was a lot of gas in his intestines. On January 31st his weight went down and for days he was gaining more weight. He stopped spitting up as much and his doctor sent me a voicemail on February 2nd to say Brayden was doing well. His weight was still up and down though.

I'd been on leave for a while and decided to go back to work since Brayden was doing better and I really wanted to stay busy to keep my mind off things. I remember being at my desk when I heard my cell phone vibrate. I stepped away and went to the break room. The doctor called and said Brayden had a few spit-ups and that his weight went up, but he'd caught an infection in his tummy. They'd given him three antibiotics and his blood count was low. She explained that Brayden was not feeling or doing well. She went on to explain that his belly had gotten bigger and with it being so big it made it hard for him to breathe. He was put back on the ventilator to help him relax. She said that he'd been diagnosed with necrotizing enterocolitis.

When she got off the phone, I stood there in the break room balling as I felt that something wasn't right. I remember weeping so hard that day. Coworkers surrounded me with love and assured me that everything would be okay. I'd never cried so hard in my life. You would've thought doctors told me my son had died. It's like God was preparing me to hear the news I would soon receive. I felt so weak at that moment as I stood there stiff. I knew I didn't have the strength to drive myself to the hospital to see him. My manager and a coworker drove my car to the hospital and dropped me off to be with my son. To this day, I'm appreciative of the love they showed me. My coworkers are literally like family.

As I entered the hospital, I ran up the stairs as fast as I could to where Brayden was. He laid there in pain with a swollen belly. I'd never in my life seen anything so painful. I couldn't believe what I was seeing. I cried so hard. My son's belly continued to grow. They had him on a high-frequency ventilator. They wanted to surgically go in and take out the infected part of the bowel. Doctors told me that they'd keep me updated on his status. As I drove home, I continued to cry. Everyone kept saying he would be fine and there were others who survived the illness. I know it is God that got me home safely that night because I was out of it. I was extremely tired and couldn't stop crying no matter how hard I tried. I remembered weeks prior, rocking Brayden and singing, "It is well with my soul… whatever my lot thou has taught me to say it is well." Out of all the songs to sing, God put that song on my heart.

I remember going home and googling success stories of children with NE. No matter how much I googled, I remembered the look in my baby's eyes when I left that hospital. He had a look on his face that said *mommy I'm tired of fighting*. I called my mom and repeatedly told her that Brayden looked tired. It's like I knew his fight would be over soon. I got a call in the middle of the night. The doctors said his belly had worsened and they needed to do an incision to look inside.

I documented Brayden's NICU journey throughout. I never imagined that there would be a final entry.

12/19

He's doing well. They stopped feeding him breast milk and went back to feedings through IVR - he wasn't digesting it as he should. He's breathing fast but they said he has to learn how to control his breathing.

12/20

They were able to take out his arterial line today. They will resume feeding him breast milk to see how he does. They will be stopping antibiotics since his numbers came back fine. His potassium is back to normal. She said that he is very active. Lol… He decided he wanted to start pulling his tubes out. They had to put them back in because he kept taking them out.

12/21

Doing well with breathing. Slow digestion with the feeding. Tummy looks fine.

Watching him closely every three hours watching to see if he gets better.

12/22

He did well with feedings. Vomited only once tonight. Tolerating feedings better.

11:15 am

Took him off the milk...back to giving him nutrients through IVR.

Will check for infection.

Put him back on antibiotics.

Inserted tube to flush out the air in his belly.

12/23

They told me he needed to be transferred to Children's Healthcare of Atlanta for further evaluation.

They believed something developed abnormally in the digestive tract.

They did additional testing today to see what's blocking digestion but we're claiming all is well.

This hospital is 100xs better. Although the drive is long, it's worth it.

They let us hold our child for the first time!

We waited on follow-up X-rays to tell us what the problem was.

They planned to do another X-ray in the morning because the contrast needed to move down.

12/24

It's Christmas Eve.

Brayden looks so cute with his Christmas hat.

He was really tired from being up all night.

His belly was nice and soft — but no stool.

Today the doctor informed us he had some not-so-good news to share. Brayden has been diagnosed with Cystic fibrosis with two mutations in gene.

By HIS stripes Brayden is healed. We prayed for total healing.

Thy will be done, Lord.

Brayden was moved on the 5th day - God's grace is sufficient for me.

12/25

It's Christmas Day!

NE doctors are everywhere.

Talked to The Cystic Fibrosis Foundation for nearly eight hours to explain Brayden's condition, the type of CF (Delta F508), and treatments.

12/26

The surgeons say okay to feed him.

GI doctors start feeding enzymes to help with digestion.

Brayden finally passed gas. YAY!

12/27

He's not ready to start feeding. They want to start enzymes which are done through apple sauce but he's not big enough to intake.

They want to be able to establish feedings and consistent weight gain.

He finally had a bowel movement.

His stool is being sent for testing. They are awaiting the GI doctors.

He is 4 lbs 7 oz.

Started on Instalyte to see how his belly tolerates it.

12/28

Few spit-ups with Instal-Lyte.

Going to give him another enema to get stool loose.

He's doing well.

12/29

Enema study

Brayden is doing great.

He had a tiny smear of poop in his diaper.

Newborn screen test for CF Blood test came back- 2 mutations.

Stool Test- numbers low

Waiting on feeding

Awaiting the sweat test

12/30

Brayden's doing well

He puked, which caused his heart rate to drop

2.21 kg 4.8 lbs Breathing very fast.

Feeding Insta-Lyte - 3 ml per hour.

Fluid through a nasal tube because of his breathing

12/31

One puke earlier from feeding Smear of poop

Weight

2.27 kg

Brayden is 5 pounds.

Want to start him with enzymes before giving him formula/breast milk.

He is breathing really fast.

Send blood test -test for infection (possibly Pneumonia)

Start him on antibiotics

Afternoon

Lab results came back fine Keeping an eye on him

They're giving him more oxygen to assist with breathing

1/1

He's doing well. Tolerating feeds just fine. No spit-ups.

Breathing pretty fast Chest X-ray

Smear in poop

1/2

Tolerating milk- 3 ml to 5 ml

Considering blood transfusions

Blood cells help carry oxygen better

Stop feeding due to spit up this morning

1/3

Start new feeding but a smaller amount

1/4

Breathing hard so increase oxygen flow to 6

Tolerating not being on his belly

Went up to 4 ml on his feeds

Still no poop — small smears

He's doing well! He finally pooped and passed gas

Not breathing as fast as he was with the oxygen

Brayden's having a great day!

1/5

Went up to 6 ml on his feeds

He's doing well

1/6

Brayden's doing well — feedings going up to 8 ml per hour

5 lbs 3 oz

2.41kg

1/7

Breathing is better

An X-ray will be done tomorrow to see if they can lower the oxygen

Increased feeds to 10 ml

Put in big boy crib

2.42 kg God says:

By HIS stripes — Brayden is healed

By HIS blood — Brayden is healed

By HIS word — Brayden is healed

Brayden is healed

Spiritually

Emotionally

Physically

Braden is healed

1/8

Up to 12 ml per hour feeds Breathing and lungs are much better

2.45 kg

1/9

2.37 kg

15 ml feedings

5 liters of oxygen has been moved down to 4 liters

1/10

Hey!!! Our boy is doing well! He's been doing well with the stools— he's gone 4 times. They are able to increase milk volume. He's breathing better.

Weight -2.39 kg

1/11

Giving him fat-soluble vitamins

He is gaining weight

The baby is doing well

Weight -2.41 kg

He's breathing really fast again

1/12

Hep B Vaccine -Agreed

High flow oxygen—decreaseflow lighter

2.55 kg Breathing better

Visit him after church! Looks great

Doc told us he'd pulled out his tubes the night before.

1/13

Doc called and said Brayden's PICC line is coming out today and his breathing has gotten tons better!

1/14

He's doing well! Got his hep B vaccine!

5lbs 6 oz

1/15

Overall he's doing well

Poop has been white — an X-ray will be done

1/16

No oxygen needed

Tolerated feeding increase

4 stools- white colored

A couple of liver function tests are elevated

Abdominal and head ultrasounds done

2.55 kg

1/17

Brayden is doing well!

Brain X-ray great

Ultrasound looked fine

Belly looked fine

Actigall for liver yesterday

Abnormal labs related to liver - Cholestasis

They started him on Actigall

1/18

No issues with his breathing. He's doing well with the medicine thus far. Increased feeds from 16 ml to 17 ml.

He didn't gain weight or lose weight - stayed the same.

They tried feeding him with a bottle yesterday but he threw it up.

1/19

Brayden is doing well! He gained weight. He took the bottle.

Which bottle does he need, again?

2.48 kg

1/20

Weight went down the night before but went up tonight when aunt Mo came to visit.

2.46 kg

1/21

2.49 kg Doing well

Brayden passed his hearing test

1/22

Doing well!

1/23

Full gastric feeds

Gi changed the formula - higher mct oil

2.6 kg

1/24

Oral skills tested

Start him on enzyme Monday

1/25

Brayden is doing well!

2.6 kg

1/26

Weight is about the same — big spit up
Starts the enzymes tomorrow

1/27

He's doing okay—not well with feeding today.

Enzymes by noon but his belly was big and he has a lot of gas in his intestines.

1/28

He's been throwing up a great bit today.

Weight loss..he spit up, pooped, and passed gas when I went to visit

Waiting for his tummy to settle from applesauce

1/29

Putting the feeding tube down further

Weight loss again

1/30

TPC feeding below the stomach is better.

He's doing so much better.

He gained 10 grams

Will re-address on the weekend.

Spit up here and there.

2.6 kg

1/31

His weight went down — going up on his feeds

Wait him out on the weekend

Start spoon of applesauce to start enzymes

Gas drops to see if it helps his belly

2/1

Stopped spitting up and belly looks good

No weight gain

2/2

Voicemail saying Brayden's doing well

2/3

Weight is still up and down

Increased calories 27

Lab tests from the liver are increasing

Vitamin K

2/4

A few spit ups

2.6 kg

Weight went up

Infection in tummy

Antibiotics

Blood count low

Brayden not feeling good

His belly has gotten bigger- making it hard for him to breathe

He's back on the ventilator to help him relax

Diagnosed with Necrotizing enterocolitis

2/5

His Belly has gotten bigger High-frequency ventilator OR take out infected bowel

Clinical status changed

Operation for development— belly has worsened

An incision on his belly to look inside

CHAPTER 8
GRACED IN GRIEF

I'LL NEVER FORGET February 2, 2020. I received a call from the doctor saying that there was nothing else they could do and that NE had destroyed his organs. He was on life support until we got there to make the decision to pull the plug.

I remember getting out of bed and beating the floor as loud as I could. "Nooo.. my baby is gone!" I can't explain what I felt. That was the worst kind of pain I'd ever experienced. My heart was broken. Brandon and I had been fasting and praying for his recovery for weeks and to hear that he wasn't going to make it…it shook me to my core.

When his father heard the news, he ran out of the house and screamed in the middle of the street. I called my mom who was devastated. She had plans to come to visit him soon in hopes he'd get better. She had my hometown Pastor call me and he prayed with us. His words were so comforting. I gained some strength from his prayer. I attempted to pull myself together as I grabbed the keys and drove us to the hospital. The look of hurt, disappointment, and pain was all over Brandon's face. We shared the exact feelings. It was the longest forty-five-minute drive ever. I began to sing *God Is* by James Cleveland as I pounded the steering wheel.

I started singing *"God is the joy and the strength of my life. He removes all pain, misery, and strife. He promised to keep me, never to leave me. He'll never ever fall short of His word. I'm going to bless and praise him in this narrow way. And keep my life clean each and every day. I want to go with Him when He comes back, I've come too far and I'll never turn back. God is, God, is my all and all."*

When we got to the hospital I felt like a walking zombie. My in-laws and friends had gotten the news and came to the hospital to be with us. I literally paced the floor back and forth for hours. I couldn't stand to see my baby in that condition. Not one other person on this earth knew the strength of my love for him. Brayden was the only one who knew what my heart sounded like from the inside. Hours later, we made the decision to pull the plug. Brandon held him for a while. I'd never seen him cry so hard. It literally tore me up inside. That was the hardest thing I've ever done— watch my child, my firstborn, my baby take his last breath in my arms. I sang *It Is Well With My Soul* as I fought back the tears. The next thing I heard was this long alarm letting us know that there was no more life in his body. That sound shook me. I couldn't believe that this was really happening. I'd carried him for thirty-two weeks, drove back and forth from the hospital for seven weeks, and literally cried out and begged God to heal his body. I had to now come to terms that he DID heal his body— just not here on Earth.

To this day I'm grateful for all the love and support that was shown to my family during that difficult time. We made the decision to have him cremated as it would be too difficult to see his lifeless body in a casket. God showed up at the homegoing celebration. Everything from the words of encouragement, music selections, and eulogy from our pastor at the time was filled with God's presence. Pastor E. Dewey spoke from the title "Solomon is on the way!" His words were, "Your Solomon can be a new business, marriage, child, job, or whatever you're believing God for is on its way." The word truly encouraged us.

The hardest part about grief is when the calls and texts stop. We had to come back home to this empty house without our son but I'm so grateful we had each other for comfort. My mom stayed with us for weeks, which meant so much. She prayed over our home and for us constantly. There was such a peace of God that dwelt in our home. Even though it hurt, we had to move forward and trust God's plan. We got counseling and therapy to help us because some days were tough.

CHAPTER 9
THE PROMISE AFTER THE STORM

WEEKS LATER, I found out I was pregnant again. When I got the news I felt a flood of different emotions— excitement, and nervousness. Months later, we hosted a virtual gender reveal (the pandemic had just started). We found out we were having a boy. The moment I found out I was pregnant, I felt like it would be a boy. I couldn't explain the excitement! We had so much boy stuff from the gender reveal. The room was already set up. After losing Brayden, the door to what would've been his room stayed shut for months.

When we got home from the gender reveal, I went to the room and wept while praising God for his grace towards us.

Brandon and I knew that we had to get our house in order. We talked about marriage and even went through couples counseling. Although I'd been taught that marriage was important and it's better to be in the will of God, I was afraid to marry again. I'd gotten comfortable with us living together after over a year, but I knew we had to do the right thing. We began to get ready for the maternity shoot a few months later. Little did I know, the shoot would turn into a marriage proposal.

He'd partnered with my best friend and they'd set it all up. I was so shocked. I still look at the photos and videos to this day in awe. Everything from my dream ring from Kay Jewelers to our outfits, to the outside scenery, and our loved ones being there to support us was priceless and beyond special. I told everyone I was down for a courthouse wedding. We were in the middle of a pandemic and I was too pregnant and not in the mood for wedding planning. My friends weren't having that! We set a date for two months later and they got to it! We got married on August 8, 2022. Eight is the number that symbolizes new beginnings. It was a beautiful day full of love and support from our families.

Weeks later, God blessed my husband and me to pay for our own semi-truck in cash. We delighted ourselves in God and he gave us the desires of our hearts. We wanted to do something in honor of our beloved late son Brayden and also create generational wealth for our future children. We'd declared that by September we would be in our own truck for business and God did it. Faith without works is dead. We got to work, sowed seeds, and made some sacrifices.

In the end, God blessed us to be loan free. God gave us the name, Overcomers Transport, which was established in September. Job 22:28 says, *When you decree a thing, it will be established for you, and light will shine on your ways.*

Not only did he bless us with the trucking company, but we also had a blessed and healthy pregnancy. As I carried our son, I prayed over us and asked God to please allow me to carry full term. For months, I drove an hour weekly to the doctor to get progesterone shots to help prevent contractions. Days closer to my due date, I had a doctor's appointment and the doctor saw that my son had grown so much that he didn't have much room or fluids, and just like that it was time to go into labor. I was admitted that evening to the hospital. When we got there they told us it would be best for me to choose the c-section option.

On November 18, 2022, I gave birth to my miracle baby, Bryson Lee Pettis. Mere words can't express the happiness that I felt on that day. I cried so many tears of joy. The day we were bringing him home, I fussed at my husband the entire trip. I was extremely cautious of my surroundings and every car around us. When we walked him into the house, it was unbelievable. I was like I'm really a mother. My son is home with me and healthy. All of Bryson's testing results came back negative for abnormalities. Even with the twenty-five percent chance for CF because of the gene his dad and I carried, Bryson was completely fine. God saw fit to show His mercy and grace toward us.

Weeks, months, then a year went by and before I knew it I had a one-year-old. I was so excited, I threw two parties for him. Some may have felt I was doing too much. I may very well have been. As far as I was concerned, I had taken a huge loss before Bryson. God blessed me with a rainbow miracle baby. I was determined to celebrate every milestone. Bryson is our "Solomon." We make it our business to anoint him and cover him with God's covenant of protection…Psalms 91.

CHAPTER 10
IT'S A MATTER OF THE HEART

GOD WILL LITERALLY ALLOW you to go through things where all you can do is trust him. I'll be honest, after losing my first-born, my faith wavered. My son passed away days after we'd just completed fasting and truth be told I didn't fast again for years.

I felt like my prayers didn't work. God started and still is rebuilding our faith daily. It's not an easy road, but it is worth it. As strong as I tried to be, I was weak. I realized over time that It was only the strength of God that was carrying me. No matter how hard I smiled,

I was literally broken and eventually, it began to impact my health. I started having chest pains for months. After several visits to the doctor and hospital, and being told it was acid reflux, I requested an X-ray.

The results showed that I had developed an enlarged heart. I was immediately referred to a heart doctor and found out my heart was functioning at about fifty percent. I was diagnosed with heart failure, severe anemia, and fluid around my lungs. When I got the news, I sat in silence for a minute and then felt one teardrop fall.

The doctor looked at me and said she was shocked by my response. She said most of her clients were hysterical when finding out they had heart disease. I felt numb. I stared at her for a few minutes as she spoke. Then I then told her, "Let's do what we gotta do." I began treatments, changed my entire diet, and took my medications. When I did the first follow-up test, my numbers hadn't changed. Ten days after finding out the diagnosis, I'd lost twenty-four pounds. What a journey it was! Some days were better than others but by God's grace, I'm still pushing through. If you know you're feeling sick and aren't getting answers please don't give up! Get a second, third, or even fourth opinion if necessary. It could literally save your life. I started posting my journey and used the following hashtags:

#**FaithOverFear**

#**IndescribableFaith**

#**WalkingTestimony**

#**HelloMyNameIsOvercomer**

#**THH**

I began to get so sick that I had to be admitted to the hospital on several occasions. During one visit I stayed for 3 days, and that was the weakest I'd ever felt. I remember calling my mom with tears in my eyes because I felt so bad. However, I continued to "put in the work" to get healthier because "faith without works is dead!" I always remembered this quote by my Bishop, "God's ability is your ability!" I worked hard at getting my health back all while trusting God.

Months later I was twenty-eight pounds down, my medications were reduced, and I got clearance to begin minimum strength training. The next echo ultrasound showed no fluid around the heart. I was grateful for the small victory. My prayer was that God would keep me focused - spiritually, mentally, and physically. Romans 8:18 was my go-to scripture and it states, *I consider that our present sufferings are not worth comparing with the glory that will be revealed in us.* I continued to post my journey for months and I switched up my hashtags:

ClaimingVictoryOverHeartDisease

#THH (Team Healthy Heart)

#BiggerPicture #LifeStyleChange

One day I listened to a sermon preached by Bishop Mitchell about seeing the bigger picture. His words stuck with me when he said, "There's a bigger picture. No matter how big or small the matter is. Lord help us to see you in it." I realized there was more to what God was doing and I shouldn't see my health journey as just a challenge. God would get the glory out of it.

As the months went by, I continued to work out and give it all I had. I went back to the doctor around March and the doctor said she didn't have to see me again until May— my blood levels and X-ray results had improved drastically. In May, I went back to the doctor to find that my heart function had improved to about seventy-five percent of its normal function. Although my heart health had improved, my mental health remained unstable.

As time grew closer to Mother's Day I struggled with the loss of my firstborn. I found myself in a very dark place. The depression was so severe that one day I literally forgot how to log into my work computer. My mind was literally blank. I was forcing myself to wake up and try to deal with life as if I hadn't been severely traumatized. I was driving by myself one day to go get something from the store. While driving, a truck swerved to another lane but the tire debris he was trying to avoid pounded into my car. I was in the car motionless and emotionless. I didn't try to stop the man or anything. I was so spaced out that I didn't even notice until I arrived at the store that he'd damaged my bumper.

After I left the store and was driving back home, the enemy whispered to me to let go of the wheel. I found myself wanting to give in and let go of the wheel. In seconds, God brought me back to myself. I pulled over at a gas station and cried hysterically. I couldn't believe what had just happened. It was at that moment that I realized I needed help. I immediately called the first two pastors that came to mind from back home... neither answered. The enemy instantly put it in my head that I was worthless and they didn't care about someone like me.

The truth was revealed when I later found out that both pastors called me back immediately but I was in a bad service area. They had both left a voice mail. One of them called me back and got through to me the second time. He prayed and gave me words of encouragement. The next morning I realized that I had a voicemail from the other pastor. I called him and had an hour-long counseling session. This was my hometown pastor who had been covering me for years. I broke down and told him EVERYTHING…things I hadn't shared with anyone. The thing I love about Bishop is that he doesn't judge and he doesn't speak unless it comes directly from God's heart. He encouraged me so much. He had me declare "God, your word is powerfully working in my life." I had to acknowledge that I needed the power of the Holy Spirit to bring me out. He left me with 3 points:

1. The power of God is working consistently and continually.
2. We have to develop a greater relationship with the Holy Spirit on a daily basis.
3. Praise God in every step of the journey.

From that one-hour conversation, I realized that it was time to activate the power that God has given us who believe in Him. I still battled for days and then realized there was a deeper level of healing that needed to take place. I went to see my OB/GYN for testing and I was diagnosed with severe depression. He requested that I take some time off from work to rest and go to therapy.

I reached out to a counselor through my job's Employee Assistance Program. I did one session with this lady and she basically told me I had too many issues for her and I needed to see a psychiatrist. I was thinking to myself, "Geesh, am I that messed up?" As time went on, I got the help that I needed through prayer, fasting, and the support of my loved ones. I looked all over for a psychiatrist, but everyone was booked up for months at a time. The time off from work did help with the healing process as I began using an app called "Calm" to help my mental state. I took a vacation by the ocean, and it brought so much peace to my heart and my mind.

I was back at work for about a month when I started having physical challenges in my body. I got off work one day, took my meds, and started feeling terrible. The room was spinning and my heart began to race. Then, I began having pain on the right side of my head, sweating profusely, and my speech began to slur. It really shook me up. I'd never experienced anything like it. I called 911 and when the paramedics arrived, they believed I was having a panic attack. The episode lasted for a few minutes and then subsided. They told me the hospitals were jam-packed due to Covid, and they thought it would be a good idea to just follow up with my doctor the next day.

The following day, I had a visit with my cardiologist and she told me she believed that what I'd experienced was a TIA (mini-stroke). She sent me to Piedmont for CT scan testing. They couldn't find anything. Although I was happy, I was confused as to what was happening to me. The episodes came back a second and third time. My blood pressure got so high the last time that I had to be rushed to Grady Hospital. I explained to them everything that had been going on with me but test after test, there were no answers. Before the doctors came in to give me the results, my cousin texted me and said to call him, we needed to talk, that God had put something on his heart.

He then called me but I wasn't able to answer because the doctors were giving me my results. When they left the room I called him back. My cousin went straight to it and said, "The reason why they can't figure it out is because it's spiritual. You've been carrying too much. Let it go! It's time to release the burden. There is a light in you and always has been. You've always been a joy to be around. Let your light keep shining. God says it's time to tell your story." I remember getting off the phone with my cousin SHOOK. I didn't even tell him that the doctors had just left my room telling me that they couldn't figure out what was going on with my speech. The nurses were getting my discharge papers ready when the head nurse came into the room. I'd never met this lady a day in my life. She introduced herself and went on to say, " I have to be obedient to God. I know you don't know me but God says he is bringing you to your knees and back to him. God is your healer. Stop giving everybody else HIS time. Stop pouring into everyone else. It's time for your cup to be filled. It's time to deal with you. The stress is causing you so much unnecessary anxiety. You've been holding on too long. Let it go." I sat there in tears, like oh my goodness.

This thing really is spiritual. I'd been running from my calling for years. In less than 5 hours, two different people who knew nothing about each other told me to let it go. You would think that was it. I called my mom to tell her about it, but before I could open my mouth to speak, she said, "God said let it go."

I was *SHOOKETH* at this point. My mom was the third person in less than twenty-four hours who told me to let it go. I was like, okay God. The third episode caused my speech to be slurred for months. I waited almost two months to begin seeing a neurologist because of how backed up they were. The neurologist explained how the overwhelming stress caused dysarthria (slurred speech). He told me that I should take it easy, especially considering that I have heart failure and I was on a lot of medicine. My prayer to God was "God, I believe you're a healer. Please correct my speech." I believe God allowed all of this to happen because he needed to shut me up so I could start writing. That was all the motivation I needed.

I'd been hard-headed for way too long. I had to realize that fear of failing is not of God. Everything I went through was preparation for what God wanted to do in my life. I had to learn from my mistakes, grow, and move forward. I will no longer allow anyone (including church folk) to convince me not to tell my story. Yes, I did that, and that too, but God still loves me and I'm proud of how far I've come. I know some will gossip about some of the things in this book, but it's my truth. God gets the glory through it. My past will no longer keep me in bondage. They don't have to gossip about it any longer. No one can tell my story the way I can!

In the words of Pastor Salters, *"Make peace with your past. What happened... happened. Move forward! God is doing a new thing. Any situation you had to pray your way out of ... you don't need to go back to."* Though I tried to run for years, when you're the one…you're the one. God will use that traumatic experience to bring him glory! I'm an example of training a child up in the way they should go and when they're older…they won't depart from God. I pray that my story has blessed you. I pray that it has encouraged you that no matter the season of life you are in, it's never too late to start over with God.

My story has been a whirlwind. No matter what I've done, God, our Father, was waiting for me with open arms to come back to him. Not only is he a loving and patient father, but he is a healer, a comforter, and a deliverer. Simply put…he is our everything! Remember, we overcome by the blood of the Lamb and the word of our testimony. I shared my testimony…now it's time for you to share yours!

I declare the old has passed away and he makes all things new. With that being said, yes my name is Andreka Walker. But allow me to reintroduce myself... Hello, my name is Overcomer! I don't claim perfection. I still have struggles but I feel like David, I'm a woman after God's own heart. I'm grateful for a new beginning in Him.

OVERCOMER

1 JOHN 5:4 (ESV)

For everyone who has been born of God overcomes the world. And this is the victory that has overcome the world — our faith

www.ingramcontent.com/pod-product-compliance
Lightning Source LLC
Chambersburg PA
CBHW070303230426
43664CB00014B/2618